So You Want to Study the Bible?

Everything you need to know about studying the Bible with LIFE on Campus and the International Christian Church

Dr. Mike Patterson

THE HOLY BIBLE, NEW INTERNATIONAL VERSION®, NIV® Copyright © 1973, 1978, 1984, 2011 by Biblica, Inc.® Used by permission. All rights reserved worldwide.

ISBN- 9798333050120

LIFE On Campus is a campus ministry sponsored by the International Christian Church (ICC). Members of the church started the campus ministry student organization to provide a fellowship for our church's students based on the Bible. LIFE stands for Living in Faith Everyday. LIFE on Campus and the ICC are non-denominational, holding to the Bible as our doctrinal standard.

Table of Contents

Introduction

On the journey to understanding Zen, one comes to find that Zen cannot simply be put into words. In other words, it's ineffable. Zen is void of thought. It is a Tabula Rasa, a blank page that is full of everything in this universe and beyond. Those words are close, but still incapable of explaining Zen. The exercise in this book is more succinct than words.

Just follow the simple directions and repeat as necessary. There is no right or wrong way to use this tool. There are no tests or quizzes afterwards. Go at your own pace. Sacred emptiness awaits you...

Made in the USA
Las Vegas, NV
04 December 2024